The Language of Birds

Kimi Sugioka

manic d press
san francisco

Some of these poems have been published in *Bombay Gin*, *Exit Zero*, *The Once and For Almanack*, *Oxygen*, *13th Moon*, and *Poems from Earth*.

The author wishes to thank Susan Dambroff, Emilia Paredes, Eleni Sikelianos, Marla Weber, Anne Waldman, Keith Abbott, and many others for their support, encouragement, and inspiration.

ISBN 0-916397-32-7
Cover Design: Tracy Cox
Distributed by Publishers Group West

These poems are dedicated to the memory of my mother.

Yes - the springtimes needed you. Often a star
was waiting for you to notice it. A wave rolled toward you
out of the distant past, or as you walked
under an open window, a violin
yielded itself to your hearing.

—Rainier Maria Rilke
Duino Elegies

Contents

A child climbs a stool
extends plump palms for washing
nowhere near the sink

Kuan Yin
Hearer of the Cries of the World

I am ear
bone and drum, I hear
thrum of flesh on flesh, squall of
babe, howl of
wolf with paw jawed in
steel musings of men, restless
in peace, peaceful in war-
silenced children into
chained-dog-whimpers

Your heart aches
in my pulse, your frail
snail self whispers
an inheritance
of laughing gulls, starling whist,
the wrist just turned
beneath the razor
meter of milklessly
lapping tongue, limping gait,
clattering beak of wounded owl
rummaging thickets with
the hopeless rustle of
a single wing

Answer, I answer
with succoring wind
and strands of hair
to wind in your fist
your infant fist
grasping at mythless roots
with grip too weak to hinder
bone-rattling snips
of judgement, lost in
skin, undone as
knots to anchors
hoisted or dropped
invisible as snowgeese
with wings turned
towards the sun

Answer I answer
with lotus
mind tuned
to cliffs scaled with
nails dug into granite
I tune my ear
to your song I
sing you
dance my
voice with peals
of joy
inform the muse
into music
of your own
arms to cradle
your own wails
in the ear
of my ear

After the Concert

On the corner of Sixth and Market
a woman is screaming
long, wordless shrieks
for loud, terrified minutes
She screams endlessly
until a man
picks her up
cradles her like
a child
As we pass she says,
I guess I just need
a little rest.

Walls

What you wake up to
once you come into
the gummy fog of morning
her tired hands nesting
one inside the other
borrowing cups of sugar
from sweeter days

What fastens the walls of night
to the walls of morning?
Sorts itself in spectrum
along the horizon?
beyond bleeding knots of scar and muscle
we keep so neatly and fetally tucked
beneath our blankets
Begging another minute
another hour of day to sleep away
yesterday's injuries

Staving off day
could become a way
of life
hobbled with yearning
for the promise of night

Between us the walls are heavy
with secrets
They moan like
broken wind-chimes
like Jericho
Take these decaying
walls away
and we will sun
flesh and spirit
at the open hearth
of our truest
home

UnNatural Selection

"[Fear of man] is not acquired by individual birds in a short time,
even when much persecuted; but that in the course of successive
generations it becomes hereditary."
                    —Charles Darwin, *The Voyage of the Beagle*

Trouble with city living is
everything tends to look Darwinian
beginning and ending with
pigeons
the way they
peck at and walk over
the wounded and sick

Trouble with Darwin
was the way he hurled lizards
into tidepools
to contrive his theories

Amblyrhynchus cristatus,
(the lizards in question)
he described as:
"hideous looking creatures
of a dirty black color,
stupid and sluggish in their movements"

Imagine that famous scientist
way out on the Galapagos
flinging lizards
to see what they'd do?

When that poor shell-shocked lizard
who'd never been transmogrified in his life
swam back to old Darwin's feet
he decided
Those lizards are just asking for trouble

And the same theory goes
for urban dwellers
More afraid of starving than those
mean city streets
Standing on the corner
at the feet of some Darwin
bewitched and amazed
at the unnaturally selective
neighborhood quota
of bad luck and death

It's a lizard mind
Flicks those channels every day of our lives
knowing it's bad, wrong, lazy and a lie
but easier than confronting the every day
that's in your face
crushing you between its fingers
like devil's food cake

Darwin chased those lizards
to the edge of a cliff
to see if they'd jump
and they wept reptilian tears
in inky nostril squirts
but they wouldn't budge
from that precipice

There's a little girl
who comes to school every day
Every day she comes to school
and won't work
and won't listen
and she is cursed into corners
and suspended for impudence

She wrote a story about why tiger roars
Snake asks why
Monkey asks why
Elephant asks, *Tiger, why do you roar
so loud at night?*

But she comes to school every day
because her home is her ocean
where her father drinks a little
too much
comes into her bedroom at night
and roars

We have a lizard brain stem
that's like a light switch
She says it flickers
on   off
on   off

so nothing gets through
that we can't handle

Family Recipe

There's not much to go on in the files.
It's a military family. Someone tells you what to do all the time.
You get married and the children start coming,
they relocate you so often you lose contact with family and friends.
After a while it's just Christmas cards and birthday presents.

He keeps the guns broken down.
He gets angry when the boys fight, sometimes he hits them.
When the yelling gets too loud she goes into the back room,
makes identical ceramic molds.
She enjoys that.

In the padded room think about how little you know of the family,
how you only see the bruise under her eye,
but only for a moment because the child brings you back.
The child lives in the present.

The room is five by six feet with carpeted walls.
Tell him, "I'm with you. You're safe."
Cross his arms over his chest, hold his wrists, lock his legs under
yours.
Rock, sing, whisper, but don't let go.
He'll say, "You're *hurting me*, you're *killing me!*"
Hold on. Keep your head tilted to one side so he can't hit your
chin.
Tell him, "I'm being careful, I'll keep you safe."

When he says he'll burn you up too,
say, "You're remembering the fire."
Don't talk too much. Say, "I'll hold you til you're calm."
He'll scream, "I *am calm!*"
Don't let go.
Don't say anything.

Wait until his breathing and heartbeat slow.
Wait until the struggling stops.
Let go one arm at a time.
Talk softly and keep your back to the door.

Hold his hand and walk him to his desk. Put a pencil in his hand,
tell him "It's time for math now."
Say, "Good, that's right, you're doing fine."
Stay with him until he forgets you're there.

At night, think about the way he collects bits of brightly colored
paper, string, broken glass. The way he calls them his treasure, his
jewels. When you take him to the beach, the way he collects so
many shells they slip through his fingers and fall out of his pockets.
When you buy strawberries, the way he puts one in his pocket for
his mother.

The way he's always hungry.
The way he brought one whole raw fish between two slices of
white bread for lunch.

Chelsea Hotel
Harry's story

Got a letter today from an old friend of mine. For twelve years we
got drunk and broke a lot of bottles together. Penny's sort of an
occult-artist-leader. I didn't hear from her for a long time cause she
was mad at me. You see I had this friend Joe who accidentally
murdered this other guy. I'm sure it was an accident. But this
friend of mine, Dan Whistler, he came into my room at the Chelsea
Hotel, grinning and yelling, "Billy Maybeck's dead!" But he wasn't
the one who murdered him. You see Dan was Jenny Whistler's
husband and she was having an affair with Billy Maybeck. But it
was my friend Joe who probably committed the murder. Someone
else found the body all trussed up and told the hotel manager. He
tried to make it to look like a natural death because he didn't want
the police coming around.

Well this other guy was going to jail for three, thirty-year sentences
so he said he'd take the rap. That was nice of him. He came from a
whole family of criminals you know and the grandmother was the
worst! She raised all these people who had a one-word vocabulary
of "Yeah." Anyway he went to jail for it instead of Joe.

Well Penny had a big mouth you know, it wasn't all just lipstick.
She got to talking big, angry at my friend who may have
committed the murder - I'm not really sure.

She sent me this postcard one time and I put a big "X" on the
address and wrote "Address Unknown" and I never heard from her
again - til today. She said she'd send me money if she knew the
right address. She knows I always need money.

So I called her up and she said she could hardly get out of bed
anymore, except occasionally, when she uses her walker. Here I am
calling her and she can't get out of bed and I can hardly walk.

Migrations

Immigrants amass
shift and suffer
on ever shore
on every continent
The way of tea
or price of rice
agitates
the sucking waves
of foreign sands

Our tongues
hooked and eyeing
needled speech
baited phrases
that fray
the delicate threads
between us

Words drift
and avalanche
while we mutely battle
mutual silencing
neither one knowing
how to bridge the burgeoning
offal and swamp
of protocol
and etiquette

Our hearts
(so rarely spoken to)
tend to wither
pale and shrivel
in the catacombs
of our migratory
nature

And still we
bravely trade
semantic madness
for mouths
open to kisses
and laughter
inching forward
belly to belly
palm to palm,
our tongues
parading
obliviously
wayward
innocent
blasphemies

Lifting the fallen rose
she said, "I was hoping
I could hang by my thorns"

Sister
for Stephanie

Hair fine roots
cleave to source
gingerly
as a butterfly
clings
to a thistle

3,000 miles
and 29 years
of beating back
bushes and brambles
for moments to spend
like pennies
like fox cubs
together

The photograph
of you at ten
in your blue velvet cape
still stings
eyes tender
with absence

Always blindly
following you
down creek paths
over river rocks
through crowds and flocks
of pigeons
in St. Mark's Square
      where I caught your breath
      between dried corn cones
      when you silvered the air
      with laughter

We sibling women
have arrived
having survived
years of shared or kept
secrets we
keep faith
in sister certainty
in unspoken poems
and kisses blown
through miles of wire
and a woman's
growing time

Synthetic Mutations
Written after the first California state execution in 26 years

No matter how hard I hammer
the gas chamber doors are barred
What my eyes see my heart
prepares to sacrifice

Hail Mary full of grace
Exorcize the ruthless prophecies
of Babylon
that sever
Magdalene from Madonna
mere from mar
mother from sea
Her babes are dashed upon the rocks
so the pious can be purified
by bathing their feet
in the blood of the wicked

Witness
a preacher lifting a street fetus
to bible light
Light a votive candle
and don't speak of dreams
wrung with the sweat of
ghostdancing samurai
temples of doom
lawnmower men

Bump and grind
bite and claw
A tepid effigy
hung with breasts and 34 year old dreams
I survived Christ's age but
still taste his tears

and store information
in megabytes that burst from my belly
like automated aliens
overriding sentience
with steel
and microchip

Butter seethes in every nook and cranny
of muffins thrown in dumpsters
denied
our moonless, emaciated children
whose hearts are caged and cut
in ritual
Take the heart out clean
Offer it to the sun
Whittle away a virgin's body
til her pulse beats into void

In Manhattan no one stops
as long as you're still staggering
but the Vietnam vet in the Picaro said
"We have no enemies
only friends who are sometimes
late."

My heart's a junkie
for a fix on reality
but it's never the same face
in the mirror
    always a trace
of you in sweat
        bleeding through my forehead

I have no lovers
only a cat who is sometimes kind
No ecstatic pill
only a straggling half-lit half-life
too conventional to stray entirely
from your remotely controlling hand
that changes channels til you come
to something extraordinary
but you never do

Witness the human beside you
who is the most amazing being
you'll ever know
before it's too late
and he's been executed
in a steel green room
after Kentucky Fried Chicken, Coke, a pack of Camels
and a bag of jellybeans

Something
a child might order
when his dream comes true

Virtual reality
is a synthetic mutation
of a still beating heart

Triple Rock

Man in stylish seagreen sweatshirt
prematurely smug mouth
sips ale
Man in wrinkled ash-grey button down shirt
lifts limpid apologetic eyes
Two large ruddy-faced women
mutter "Red Rock" to potbellied bartender
who turns to me sarcastically, says
"Don't look so excited"
twirls a beer glass high in the air
catches it, notices the crack, throws it
away
Scrawny under-aged looking youth
slams dirty mugs in suds, says
"Ready for another?"

On the sidewalk, perched on ledges, abandoned daytime tables
or flat out on the cement
homeless men pass a cigarette
discuss night-wanderings
plead for change
A bear-shaped man stomps towards me
stops, growls, hisses, stomps on

My companion is angry
because I have studied every face but his
I try to explain how the problem is as much in the bar
as in the street
how each is obliviously trapped
in their own dilemma
but he doesn't hear me
can't step outside of his own
face

Pretty Woman

I am not a pretty woman
a fine woman
or a milk and honey woman
and I will not stand at the end of a long line of women
you have tried to hit on, flatter, cajole or fuck
You have done enough flirting
to fill a millennium
with nickel and dime
lies and bribes

I am not a pretty woman
and if you want me to
make time for you
flirt with my soul

But don't mess with me
cause it'll be
too bad
You'll wake up and decide
you don't like my
nose or my thighs
and my passion
will dry up
quick as spit
on a hot griddle

I am an ugly woman
When I get up in the morning
I grind up old lovers' bones
in my cereal
When I bleed I need
privacy, comfort
a little hot tea and a back rub
and I still might run you
out of the house

I am not a pretty woman
I have pimples and don't like to
do laundry or keep house
I like to sit back
smoke a cigarette
and let someone else clean up

You come into my place of birth
and name it cunt or snatch or pussy
You name me what you want
when what you want is in one place
or other places where I am not
You can't tell me
from who you are
for who I am
from what you want
when what you want
isn't me
because I'm not who or what
you think I am
OR
that I'm not anyone at all
that I'm unacceptable

You think you can make me be
what you want
where you want
anytime you want
me to be there I
won't be there I
will be where I
want you here
where I want you all over
I want you to want me all over
If you don't I won't let you
take me where my birthplace is
sacred my
place of birth where
you were born
from womb-world
from womb-mind my
hands caress a child

caress a sister
caress your arms your
face your
sex caress your
palm your left side your
right ankle
and you say FUCK
you say CUNT
like it's war and you scored
one more gook
one more exotic
pin up girl

You are the child
your mama grew inside her,
say,
didn't she teach you
we are all the same woman?
The same woman
you burned
at the stake?

At the stake
you learned to say
witch, whore, cunt, bitch, dyke
We learned to say
wop, faggot, nigger, spic, kike
You learned
to trade names
that enslaved you for
names
to enslave me
Vain names make dangerous games:
AIDS, unwanted babies, suicide, genocide
I say it's time to
re-educate ourselves
before the earth dies
from her
babies cursing her
milk dry

You say fuck but
you don't mean fuck
you mean me and
you mean womb you
mean you want to
conjure a baby?
Or at least bear
this love out inside me
not outside me
not outside you
in some nameless, faceless, birthless
cunt or fuck place
not in some
inanimate
magazine place

I am not a pretty woman
I am a beautiful woman
who stands with hands open
No matter how many times you
sell me out or turn me in
I will win
myself back from you
I will turn tables, shill cards and teach children
til cows come home and you find
some worthy words to call me
and there will be
no more need
for this poem

Remember
summer
plums
windfallen
apples
the sound of
fruit
walking?

Ancestral Sestina

My grandmother was grown in Matsuyama castle
She played the koto
never learned to cook
was a plum blossom child
plucked from a young tree
to marry her sister's widowed husband in America

She grew ten children in America
in California where her home was his castle
watched him graft plum branches to an apricot tree
reminded of the koto
she played as a child
when she wasn't learning to cook

Her daughters learned to cook
hamburgers and tsukemono, American
names for every child
At times she grew distant in the hum of her mind-castle
cried for her koto
clung to her plum tree

Twice felled from her tree
plum rendered with cooking
she surrendered the strains of her koto
to foreclosure by the Bank of America
She burned Matsuyama photos of her rice-paper castle
escaped to Colorado as the camps claimed her children

Roosevelt's imprisoned, epicanthic-eyed children
grew tough and cordial as manzanita trees
grew rock gardens around barren barrack-castles
determined to cook
the meatless bones tossed off by America
without snapping the back of the koto

I have never held a koto
am not a child
of assimilated America
am the apricot branch of the plum tree
an ambivalent cook
in a negligent castle

I imagine the poignant strain of a koto, tuned to the ear of a
paper-walled castle
a petulant child, in need of a cook
who planted a plum tree in the Salinas valley

Relations

Basho admired moonflowers on his way to the deep north. In her garden, my aunt points out the prickly globe that blooms at night. Tomiko, child of bountiful harvest, in the year of the windfallen outhouse.

Coyote ghost looms
behind the english elm
How spare this winter sun

"The wandering jew is from the Fletchers, the succulent from Mrs. Manzanola, and the octopus plant is from 1231 Locust Street. The people have died so I feel I must keep the plants alive."

O shattered pumpkin
Jack o'lantern grin shivers
face down in the stream

Basho walked the narrow road in sandals and a paper coat. My samurai ancestors sold their title five hundred years ago. Their sword keeps its edge in my father's house.

"Dad's carving the turkey. He wasn't too happy when I backed into the Jaguar.
Dad's carving the turkey, the house is full of Blums, I'd better go..."

Rabbit in the larkspur
Rabbit in the moon springs clear
Tempering the sword

After the guests leave we eat
shoyu on our pickles, green tea over
white rice, shoyu on our turkey.
My uncle comes home with
blood on his hands, smiles
at his wife, hides
the bird.

Geese stay low after
the moon sets, knowing better than to
fly in the face of the sun

After waking from her nap, my aunt
throws a slipper on the stomach of her still
sleeping husband. His eyes open, undaunted he feels for the soft
blow, solemnly examines her tiny
sole, as though he had been waiting for this shoe to drop.
Retired shoemaker of 43 years.

Basho cries for long dead
warriors, leaves the baby
on the road to die

Sun-webbed flecked
memory: "Grandfather chose a sturdy tree for grafting
one fruit to another - Miraplum?
I don't know - some well-rooted thing..."

Chartreuse fin slices
rippled lake under withered
frown of muddy sky

"Grandmother loved the fields
hated the indoors - maybe that's why
she hated to cook
but she cooled the baked fish
in the bathtub so the flesh
would remain on the bone
to please us..."

Moonflower, larkspur
eleusis, columbine draw
straws, wander the sun

Write, He Said

I write

                without knowing
     who

          I
am

        or what

        I will be

    when the pen

       webs its way Orpheic

down or into

     scarlet or chartreuse

iris or sweet pea

       rare as honeysuckle
                   in winter

What wields
         a poem open

wills
       androgyny
        anarchy
          symmetry,

or a dark, dark bruise
   on the heart

Literati

    can't spare

the price of bread, milk and sugar

             can't quell

      the mulching

    of internal

    Implosion

           "Poetry is

                    the language
      of the human soul"

she said

    I said

I've got
no time to fill
my poem quota
the supervisor's
a cricket
in my ear:

      "Emit no evil"
he says
      "live on time"

    I've got one eye
           on the page
      and one
on the clock

A Harvest of Stars

Dawn's tourniquet binds my jaw
winds down a blind and empty street
argues in strains of apple and oak
that measures
the burning abyss between us

There is no fortune beyond the touch of our fingers
Beneath the cloud of your brow I come
sheathed in veils of tourmaline and quartz
my hand my only
weapon
my only gift
What treasure of pulse and flesh do you bring?
Like the Roshi who saw my tears among a hundred sightless
disciples
none other but you can see me
None other but you
can save me
from the wreck and drone
ploughed in our blood
that disdains the reclamation
and purge
of embrace

I cannot erase our tainted ways
but for you I would shatter
the shaping cell of memory,
unfold my wildest feather
for ephemeral journeys into divine jungles
where we could hunt and pray our sins into scripture
whisper Lucifer's secrets out of our bodies and into the ether
to illumine the thousand masks of raped vision
and flay them with Erato and Calliope

Companions of the flame
make with me an odyssey
and we might fly
into the crystal womb of a phoenix
our hearts all wile and wing

Pouring
for Susan

It's been a long
day, you look
tired, would you like
a cup
of tea?

I can see
by the lines around your
mouth, eyes, color
of your skin
is pale
is white
is the color of
votive candles in
Spain, in the
churches there were
glass cases with
wax effigies
of saints
of virgins
dead or sleeping
arms filled with
roses, wearing
satin
smiling, you look
like them, you must
be very
tired, have a little
more tea

One morning at school
Maurice came in
growling, yes
growling and looked like he might
bite
and locked himself in the
bathroom while his teacher
stood outside the door saying,

"Having a hard morning, Maurice?
Looks like you're having a hard morning.
Looks like you might need some
tea. Why don't I fix you
a nice cup of
tea?"

There was something
in her voice
that was soothing
that was
careful as
balancing eggs on her
tongue and she
made him
tea and he grew
calm
and wanted to add
and subtract
for her

I used to throw
parties, invite
friends, prepare
chicken with
feta cheese and
spinach, pies
apple and ricotta
and afterwards
I'd say,
"Tea, anyone?"
and I'd steep and grind
pour and say,
"Are you full?
Are you well?
Would you like
some more?"

I pour and it's
enchanted pouring
from long years of
practice, centuries of

sentiment, the
sediment of ancestry
I cannot recollect
but have taken up
like dandelion seed takes root
once the child has
made her wish, so
temporal, it shines on her cheek
for a wingbeat

But I've forgotten
it's tea you're wanting
I'll do the pouring
I've always done the pouring
See how the leaves remain in the cup?
See how I read them
with my eyes
closed?

The Sparrow Whose Tongue Was Cut Out
for Emilia

A house sparrow
billows her body with breath
and surrenders rapture

A woodsman found her wounded
brought her home to convalesce
His wife grew jealous of her song
and so cut out her tongue

We blaze
a trail cut in tongues
broken with yearning
for the sensate song
of the wild

Wise desires plague our dreams
endless doors to claimless territories
The feral scent is keen upon us
We've lost our nature and have
no way to follow

But because we are creatures
of passion and promise
because we believe in the impossible
we barter:

for the child a viper strikes
out of an unrequited love
of innocence

for Europa whose honey-scent
betrayed her

for them who venture into Hades
to unravel raptures of the deep
in sweet liquid lullaby

Love, liebe, believe
in gods with feathers, fetlocks and claws
We've lost our nature and have no way to follow

Saints and seraphim
are tiresomely pious
They envy
our sordid self-absorption
our tactile reality
our terrible desires
We must mix and mate to create
a bestial divinity

Believe in wildness
brave the savage angels
breathe sweet tobacco and
answer the razors keening
by dancing with the sun
in a stand of cottonwood
to retrieve the sparrow's song

Love Poem

Love is all down with me
a drowned sailor on leave
No glance or smile casual
never a date or interlude
always a crack in the sky or mantle

I never dream of other lovers
never want anyone other
than who's beside me
there is no one else
only you only you

Some beauty and some beast
imprisoned in our bodies
searching for beauty and
craving the beast
for it's they who remember
the notes of the lyre

I have drowned in the mouth of a lover
in the mouth of my mother
in the home of my father
in dogwood, rhododendron, saffron
chili pepper, jewelweed, sage
sourwood honey and sweet white corn

while a miserly muse
nods
five fat visions
Every night she counts her rings:
ruby, sapphire, amethyst, emerald
She permits my gaze
now and again
when she lets down her guard
like a mule or
borderline case

She says I am evil:
Eve, Lilith, Inanna, Kali
a child filching cookies
is easily greedy
for wet
guilt embedded
dreams

But I say love
is necessary maelstrom
and we must embrace the love:
of old men in cigar stores
or loud, laughing girls who
suck candy and strut down Divisadero Street
of boys on skateboards, secretive and high
of uncles who shoot doves and crack open walnuts for squirrels
of fathers faded from work and worry
or mothers who love their babies
but crave crack
of soldiers who fight because only the military
readily employs impoverished men
of boys who kill cause they expect to be killed
by the time they're eighteen

The love of a woman who marries a bear
of a man who marries a buffalo
Love of sacred flaws:
the scar on your wrist
your reckless mind
love of candor, audacity,
plurality,
revolution and tradition

People may be trivial
but human exchange is not
Every time we curse a clerk
or threaten a child
we violate ourselves
Every time we walk out the door
we have to barter our way
back home
Every smile or condemnation

is a light or needle
in someone's cerebellum
We must learn to love like a redwood or white oak
that just digs in
and grows towards the light

Untitled*

Be gone before the door closes
like the child who begins a fresh
painting before the last one is dry
For among her hundreds
there is none so enduring
as the one beneath her brush
and only in the hands of a child
will the colors survive

Forget death
Hear the song that carries
above the crashing waves
the same storm music
that crushes the sailor
cleans the sand

* Permutation of Rilke's *Thirteenth Sonnet to Orpheus*

Ethnopoetics

I have almond eyes and a full moon face and
you want me quiet and three steps behind
with my honey-almond skin
and my eyes full of moons
my Scots-Irish tongue and Cherokee grin
my mouth is open and I'm always talking
and you say, "You don't seem Japanese"

I carry a Zuni fetish to remind me of who I am not
I wear Gypsy skirts and lavender kimonos
with eyes like almonds and my face a full, yellow moon
I come from your reservations

I prefer tortillas to fishcakes
apple pie to pickled plum
With my smoked almond eyes and moonfilled face
you would have me Hawaiian, Eskimo, Mexican, Navajo
you would have me of some finite origin
so I must always circle "other" under "race"

I wear Chinese slippers and make a good chicken soup
I study African dance and dream in Greek
With my almond eyes and full moon face
I will always remind you of who I am not

Don't Go Near The Window

don't go near the window
a mother says to her
10 or 11 or 12
year old son

Maybe he was eating popcorn and watching
Nightmare on Elm Street
Maybe he was playing nintendo or
arguing with his brother bout who was
better at basketball
Maybe he was watching his sister
nurse her baby
whose father had gang-banged
his way to an 18 year old grave

Don't go near the window
Stay over here with me in the back bedroom
did you hear me boy?

One night I counted 6 shots
1-2-3-4-5-6
shots on the freeway
and waited
for the screech of tires
scrape of metal
break of glass
that didn't come
but I held my breath
just the same

You have to stay away from the window
when boys are so tortured
they drive around shooting at anyone
at everyone
trying to get someone
to pay attention

Don't go near the window
his mother says and he's a good boy and
obeys, backs away and waits by her side
his 10, 11, or 12 year old heart cartwheeling
with curiosity
because he doesn't yet understand
about mortality and when
the shooting stops he waits a long time
at least a minute
or a lifetime

When the bullet strikes
we wonder how he felt
his young wired mind firing
neurons and poems
we'll never know
because death is such a curious customer
and an adolescent boy is programmed
to look out the window
because that's
how he learns
what to do
to survive

Bartender

I left the party to have a cigarette at the bar. The bartender was friendly, asked me what I did for work. He was impressed that I was a teacher. (This only happens with people from other countries.) When it's his turn he says,

> "I came from Cambodia fifteen years ago. My mother and father are dead, sisters and brother, dead. I got a good job now, the owner's a good guy. I got a little girl five years old, she says, 'Daddy, you're so messy, you leave your shoes on the floor.' I can't explain to her that I can't worry about that now. I think I'll always leave my shoes on the floor."

Military Mite

I thought Jim had an attitude when I saw him smoking and jiving in the club car. Snub-nosed, short boy-man of 23 with a tan kerchief tied round his head and a black, silver-studded cowboy hat on top. I played my songs and Jim played *Stairway to Heaven* three times (it's the only song he knows on guitar). He plays piano and wants his own band and songs but has trouble writing lyrics. He bullied me into writing a verse to this four chord number he'd work up. When I sang them he became my friend for life.

After awhile he explained the kerchief. Turns out he's an army man, stationed in Fort Riley. He enlisted at 19, nothing else to do without money for school and no prospects. He ended up in the Persian Gulf where he was wounded by a scorpion. Couldn't figure how that hell-creature climbed up the tank and into his bedding.

After he got back to the U.S. he was in a tank when a fire alarm went off. When he scrambled for the hatch his partner, who was outside, turned the gun to clear the passage. Because he's small, he was halfway through when his head got caught in the turret. It tore off both ears. That was when I saw the stitches beneath the scarf.

He said it was all for the best cause his ears stuck out bad before, and the army was providing extensive plastic surgery to make them look right. He was glad he was enlisted cause they were taking such good care of him.

When my stop came he carried my guitar to my seat, gave me his address and kissed my hand. As I got off of the train I silently wished him a fistful of musical, warless dreams and a perfect pair of ears.

Double Dutch

On buckling playground asphalt:
candy wrappers
pink bunny barrettes
headless plastic monsters
bow shaped buttons
melting bubble gum
donut skid marks
used condoms
and bullets

A salamander
(at first mistaken for a bug)
is ecstatically fondled by fifty-four
nature deprived
six year old
hands
until it is finally
loved to death

No slides
jungle gyms
swings
tunnels
wooden bridges

but beneath three
netless, graffiti covered backboards
child ghosts
sweat & swear
pound hoops
haunt the streets
fill shopping carts with aluminum cans
or hover about liquor store transoms
where their supple bodies
succumbed to the gun

while our youngest
valiantly continue
to play:
kickball
four square
double dutch
hopscotch

How many little girls
sent to the store for ice cream
survive
behind-the-dumpster rapes?

How many little boys from
this overcrowded
understaffed
quota driven
text deprived
elementary school
outrun the cold metal
drop top
speaker bump of
this street slumped
tomb?

At 8:10 AM
eleven year old Damian says,
Life stinks, Miss Kimi,
I wish I was dead

Dante tells me
he's going to run away from home
leaves me three suicide notes
in as many weeks
This time, you'll never see me again...

Pigeons coo, tires screech
sirens follow gunshots
and 2 inch obituaries
follow hapless youths
on the wrong street
at the wrong time

where all the streets
are the wrong streets
all the time

Outside the smoke-filled
shit scented
teachers' lounge
boys plot to steal a
cellular phone
Two mothers
duke it out in the hallway
tripping
over kindergartners
desperately trying to maintain
the straight silent line
Mrs. Miley
worked so hard
to perfect

Seminary gang
14th Street gang
claim school doors, walls
and bathroom windows
Their determined signatures defeat
every apathetic
district whitewash
and we dread the night
when they will accidentally meet
on this last, greatly coveted, open
space

At 8:20 AM
a task force
of 15 plainclothes police
with rifles
surround the blue house
across the street
as the children are frantically
hustled inside
without breakfast
without baths

My mom was shot in the leg
last night
My auntie was taken to jail
My mom wouldn't let me in
so I slept in a van

An entire third grade class becomes hysterical
when a student describes
his cousin's drive by death
on their way to school
and a stumbling substitute asks
Who here has known
someone who has died?

I can't remember how many brothers, cousins,
fathers and uncles were killed this year
but I'm learning
how to skip fast
between the ropes
and keep on
jumping

Why Riot?

The boy lives in the projects with his mother and sister
Hungry for sugar and a new pair of Nike's
He came to school the day after he was raped
tried to sing along with Michael Jackson
I can still see his broken child's body
hear his spirit
snap

Desert Storm's on like a mini-series
The fly boys go off to fight
sanitized military missions
It's like nintendo
but more exciting
They come home to lay-offs and lies
about a man
beaten in the street
on video telecast
three times a day

Smug State Senators
badger a woman
about whether she was sexually harassed
Live in D.C.
she defends her virtue
on every station
in a nation where their relations
were once enslaved
her accused takes his place
as Supreme Court Justice
He is bought and she is sold

LA's the city of freeway marksmen
and "drive-by shootings"
is a household phrase
but even LA can't deny the video eye
that reveals state & street secrets
on candid camera

Newscasts revise rebellion
into repeated brutal beatings
of a lone white man
ravaged window displays
toilet paper lootings
empty Nike shelves
pampers and pepsi piled high in the streets

In Southcentral a boy
was scared and sick on orange soda
In streetsmart reckoning
he figured it was time to leave
Even a nine year old can read
between the scriptures of LA Law
His mother reported jobless throngs
filling the streets
milling and cussing
the last vestige of justice
spat back in their faces
by the lip smacking spittle
from a Grand Wizard's wet red mouth

As we pitch and reel
in the propaganda shackles of TV duality
we count our blessings like sheep
and dream in sphinx-like riddles:

*What walks on two legs in the morning
and 10,000 at night?*

*What is the difference between
a riot and an insurrection?*

Road Poem:
California to Colorado

Oakland

The rose bush in my garden
strides towards me
with yellow fists

Baby birds cry
from their nest in the porch eaves
I worry one
I worry one will
I worry
one will fall
out

Highway 40

Suffering from two kinds
of impaired vision
what we seek
is a cure
for eyes and dreams

I had almost forgotten
how to steal a field of lilies
with just a glance

Arizona

Canyon de Chelly

Cottonwoods
russian olives
tamarisks & chollas
prickly pear bristle emerald
against swirling red
canyon walls
Black scar on white cheek
Moon through cottonwood branches

New Mexico

Chaco Canyon

Waxwing, bushtit twitter
sun charms its way
through warm heaven morning
Green and yellow striped beetle
won't let go of my sweater
without a good fight

Jemez Springs

In the youth hostile
on my bed
A tooth!

I complain
about heat, coyotes, bugs
muddy roads, lightning, dust
Susan
sleeps

Ojo Caliente

Even the sky
feels abandoned

We bathe sun from our skin
sing into night
with honey and sage breath
blow notes through the bones
of our ancestors

Trussed lovers in a hammock
answer one another
in breath

Wine-red sunlit throat
A hummingbird pirouettes
in mid-air

Abiqui

Ghost Ranch Living Museum

Roadrunner, prairie dog, coyote, raccoon
bald eagle, golden eagle, mexican wolf
kestler, cougar, black bear, skunk
great-horned owl, red-tailed hawk
beaver, gila monster, red fox, elk

all wounded by humans
all caged

For bald eagle I will kiss the wind
For coyote, greet his brothers
For hawk my songs will soar
For fox I will speak articulately
For beaver, honor trees
For cougar, bask on a high rock
For skunk I will be audacious
For kestler I will mind my dress
For black bear, care lovingly for my children
For elk, walk the Rockies
For golden eagle I will tell stories
For gila, love the earth
For owl, sing to the moon
For raccoon I will maintain an affectionate nature
For roadrunner, travel
For prairie dog, build a strong community
For the last wolf I will mourn

Our Lady of the Desert Monastery

Cliffs streak red, amber, chalk, pewter
Thunder barks down canyons
Rio Chama gurgles downwind
You can hear it if you meditate
or try to

At prayer time
a ring-necked dove
flutters against the chapel windows

The chapel is empty
silence is huge
Missing monks worry the guests

I comb my hair by canyon light
feathered folk fly by
2,4, 20 at a time
Morning glory blooms purple
by rusting wagon wheel
A face stares up
from a stone

Raton

25 modern gas stations
21 restaurants
12 motels
2 campgrounds
1 museum

Colorado

Trinidad

What kind of pie do you have?
Banana cream, just made last night
It's very good
the dishwasher ate six pieces

Local History

Jesus Maria Garcia
"known for his unfailing goodness and
cleanness from the taint of badness"

The DiRago brothers
"did unlawfully and willfully
keep open on the Sabbath day
a tippling house
in which spirituous vices
and vinarous liquors
were then and there
kept for sale"

"That hanging was half an hour late"
"Yeah, the sheriff and the condemned man
got to talking about their bicycles"

Denver

In the garden
Dora is amazed
at the prayerful petals
of a closed lotus

The priest is muddled
when god and buddha
spit on their hands
and shake

Midwifery

Enter girlchild
      pebble and bass-filled stream
Enter boychild
      playing with breath
          and faulty continent
She fleeces her cave with phlox, spanish moss, rose petals
     she lies down, listens
         watches him cull melody
            from wind and crow rustle

Enter woman
      caterpillar climbing
          leaf after leaf
Him with satchel, with bouquet, with pacemaker
     Turning amber she turns grey, turns black
He carries her from sunlight, down shafts, mines, rattler pits
     She bides time, carries
        his child, licks
          her cubs, leaps
from precipice to kitchen counter, waits
     for his offerings:
wood, deer liver, mountain goat
     Her torn linings, shredded countenance she
        sprinkles in soups, porridges, she
          lies down, tired
    wind climbs canyon walls
      whistles her to sleep

Enter man with blue suit askew he
     throws coat and newspaper, calls
        her to the kitchen, chides
         her for sleeping, wants
           feeding
Preparing the ewe she listens to his
     surgical disasters, rubs
        salts, marjoram, takes
          a long time with the salad and rice

Ladle slips, hits a missed tumor, he
        throws his shoes
                one after another, climbs
                        inside her
                                rose hips

She rides southbound trains
        carries sand in her shoes
                scribbles scripture, recipes
        for acid and alkaline, her hair
                wound in bright winter ribbons, her
                babe tucked in the crook of her arm, she
                        withstands the gavels of winking judges
                                denies herself bread and jam
                                        denies
her corsage, her garter, her glass of sherry, her nine sundry lives,
she
                scavenges dumpsters, prowls
                        boulevards for tricks, decides
                                which baby to feed
                                        which
                                to turn away

She speaks Pious, "You will be converted to a worthy man."
or Whorish, "I will take you anyway, confine my price to demand."
or Motherly, "Find a good woman to take up the handwork I
began
        but never a wife,
                never a wife to thread you
                        any other way."

She who names me is being born
        heralding news of old wives tales:
                mistress, seamstress, princess
                waitress, schoolmarm, midwife

She is coming
        between my breasts
                pushing husbands and urchins aside
I wedge Circumference between my knees and climb
        rockface, crater, mesa, skyscraper, winged
                in name only

She is coming
      who must have melon at daybreak
      who savors morsels of jam, she
          of the chime and orange peel
      Her two fine strong daughters
          her clock wound to interior pulse
              she addresses the future in present tense,
shuttles
                yarn into dream in one motion

She of I who know her wet or wrung out to dry in the sun
She of ochre, peach, brine and periwinkle
She of helmet and scythe who scours skillets and shakes gourds
She of warty countenance, sallow-skinned embrace, furrowed navel

She is coming who rants with breasts exposed
      her hymen no longer probed she sails
          for Greece, Denmark, Japan
She takes northbound trains despite the crooked spines
      of husbands and sons climbs
          but does not name mountains
             weds the snowgoose, treads
                a threadbare wedding carpet
                  azalea, camelia
                    her trousseau
She is India ink from jars and wells
      spilled onto your vellum, your gabardine
          trousers, fine panama hat
She is patriot and rebel
   her name invisibly carved beside mine
She carried
   your duties, your child, your long-tongued name to her grave

My blossom
my fruit
I am fire-born and labor-weary
I cannot reclaim your practiced eye
but my womb is an infinite basket
where I bear the s/he of I
of scallop and locket
naked and humming
over and over
again

The Language of Birds

Ask the stones
how your desires
could have snapped
the backs of winged creatures
flocking to some other
heat
unregistered
in this armored
unrequited
grammar

Spidering along
       some soft pink moan
       some grunting shame
you shaved from your head
in a pillow of night
where you reclined
for an instant

       til a falling maple leaf
       disturbed you

       til the threads of a cobweb
       bound you

       til a meadowlark's song
       troubled you

All this
endangering
the last translator
of the language of birds
who breaks in the moment
between the slap and the child's cry
for you who long
to answer

manic d press

publications

Signs of Life: channel-surfing through '90s culture.
   edited by Jennifer Joseph & Lisa Taplin. $12.95
Beyond Definition: new writing from gay & lesbian san francisco.
   edited by Marci Blackman & Trebor Healey. $10.95
Love Like Rage. *Wendy-o Matik* $7.00
The Language of Birds. *Kimi Sugioka* $7.00
The Rise and Fall of Third Leg. *Jon Longhi* $9.95
Specimen Tank. *Buzz Callaway* $10.95
The Verdict Is In. *edited by Kathi Georges & Jennifer Joseph* $9.95
Elegy for the Old Stud. *David West* $7.00
The Back of a Spoon. *Jack Hirschman* $7.00
Mobius Stripper. *Bana Witt* $8.95
Baroque Outhouse / The Decapitated Head of a Dog. *Randolph Nae* $7.00
Graveyard Golf and other stories. *Vampyre Mike Kassel* $7.95
Bricks and Anchors. *Jon Longhi* $8.00
The Devil Won't Let Me In. *Alice Olds-Ellingson* $7.95
Greatest Hits. *edited by Jennifer Joseph* $7.00
Lizards Again. *David Jewell* $7.00
The Future Isn't What It Used To Be. *Jennifer Joseph* $7.00
Acts of Submission. *Joie Cook* $4.00
12 Bowls of Glass. *Bucky Sinister* $3.00
Zucchini and other stories. *Jon Longhi* $3.00
Standing In Line. *Jerry D. Miley* $3.00
Drugs. *Jennifer Joseph* $3.00
Bums Eat Shit and other poems. *Sparrow 13* $3.00
Into The Outer World. *David Jewell* $3.00
Asphalt Rivers. *Bucky Sinister* $3.00
Solitary Traveler. *Michele C.* $3.00
Night Is Colder Than Autumn. *Jerry D. Miley* $3.00
Seven Dollar Shoes. *Sparrow 13 LaughingWand.* $3.00
Intertwine. *Jennifer Joseph* $3.00
Feminine Resistance. *Carol Cavileer* $3.00
Now Hear This. *Lisa Radon.* $3.00
Bodies of Work. *Nancy Depper* $3.00
Corazon Del Barrio. *Jorge Argueta* $4.00

Please add $2.00 to all orders for postage and handling.

manic d press
box 410804
san francisco ca 94141 usa
distributed to the trade by publishers group west